Nottingham Inns and

on old picture postcards
Volume 2

David Ottewell

THE ALBERT HOTEL,
DERBY ROAD,
NOTTINGHAM.
Telephone No 806.
Telegrams:
Albert Hotel, Nottingham.
Family and
Commercial Hotel.
MISS JONES,
Proprietress.

1. The Albert Hotel - Derby Road, Nottingham. An advertising card for this impressive building near the junction of Parliament Street and Derby Road. A popular meeting place, it was extended in the 1930s with a new wing and Scotch Bar. It was demolished to make way for the Inner Ring Road in 1970. This card was sent from Nottingham to London in April 1913.

ISBN 978 1900138 14 7

£3.95

Designed and published by
Reflections of a Bygone Age,
Keyworth, Nottingham
First published 1996, reprinted 2009

Printed by
Adlard Print & Reprographics Ltd,
Ruddington, Nottingham

Front cover:
Ferry Boat - Stoke Bardolph. A superbly composed card published by Nottingham firm C.& A.G.Lewis which was sent from Netherfield in 1926. It shows how close the inn was to the River Trent and explains why it has received flood damage on a number of occasions. The ferry went from opposite the inn and until a few years ago was operated by George Chambers, who charged 6d.

Back cover (top):
The Rose and Crown - Cotgrave. The name derives from the 15th century, and shows respect for both county and monarchy. Apart from a porch on the front door and new signs, the pub looks similar today. This postcard dates from the 1920s.
Back cover (bottom):
The Plough and Waggon and Horses - Halam. Two pubs on the same card published by A.W.Bourne of Leicester in the 1960s. The post office has now moved around the corner and at the time of writing the 'Plough' is up for sale for conversion to a private residence. The 'Waggon and Horses' dates from 1752 and like many older pubs used to have its own brewhouse.

2. Sawyers Arms - Lister Gate, Nottingham. Advertising home-brewed ales, the 'Sawyers Arms' can be seen just to the right of the Walter Memorial Fountain on this 'Peveril Series' card of 1904. Three doors up is the more impressive 'Caledonian Hotel'. This card was used to send birthday greetings to a friend in Kent.

Introduction

After the church, the pub or inn has for many years been the focal point of village or community life. Before the days of television and video, the majority of people's entertainment had to be 'self' made. The village pub or inn provided a convivial gathering place in which it was possible to forget about the troubles of the day.

Unfortunately, changing styles and fashions have resulted in alterations to traditional pubs and inns. Many independently owned inns have proved uneconomic and have either been swallowed up by large brewery chains or closed altogether. Even the larger breweries have closed many smaller pubs in pursuit of profit. If not closed, large numbers of pubs have fallen prey to so-called modernisation. Some would argue that in going through this process, much of their character has been destroyed. The changing of many traditional pub names is particularly to be condemned.

Postcards are an invaluable reference source to remind us of pubs and inns in the days gone by. Since 1902, when postcards as we know them today (with a picture on one side and the message and address on the other) were introduced, almost every theme imaginable has been illustrated on a card. Both local publishers like Albert Hindley in this 'Clumber' series and national firms such as Frith of Reigate and Valentine of Dundee produced views of even tiny villages. A considerable number of these postcards included a view of the local inn. It is from these cards that the pictures in this book are chosen.

My hope is that this second selection of Nottinghamshire pubs and inns will provoke many fond memories and will encourage people to try to preserve our remaining 'character' public houses.

David Ottewell
September 1996

Parliament Street (showing Samuel Morley's Statue), Nottingham

3. Turf Tavern - Upper Parliament Street, Nottingham. Central to this picture, 'The Turf Tavern' has undergone two significant changes this century. It was demolished and rebuilt in 1923, and at the time of writing, it has just been renamed 'The Samuel Morley', taking its name from the subject of the statue seen in the foreground. Card published by Valentine's of Dundee about 1912.

4. The George Hotel - Nottingham. This pre-World War One advertising card shows the impressive establishment built in 1820 on the corner of George Street. Reflecting its status, it attracted a respected clientele, including in the summer of 1852 the novelist Charles Dickens.

MISS KNILL, MANAGERESS. THE GEORGE HOTEL, NOTTINGHAM.

MILTON STREET, NOTTINGHAM

5. Old Corner Pin - Upper Parliament Street, Nottingham. Standing at the junction of Clumber Street, Milton Street and Parliament Street, the 'Old Corner Pin' was a very popular pub. Seen here on a 'Peveril Series' card (No.219) posted in 1912, it was selling Home Brewery Co. ales. Sadly, in recent times it has been gutted and turned into a shop.

6. Horse and Groom - St Peter's Square, Nottingham. At the head of Lister Gate can be seen the 'Horse and Groom Hotel'. It was from the outside of these premises that many of the horse-drawn buses and trams started their journeys. Card in the 'Reliable' series published by William Ritchie.

Dining Saloon, "Horse & Groom" Hotel, St. Peter's Square, Nottingham
Luncheons, Dinners, Teas, Suppers, &c.   Chops & Steaks from Silver Grill.   Parties catered for.   Tel. 3674.

7. Dining Saloon - Horse and Groom - St Peter's Square, Nottingham. This advertising card, posted in Nottingham in 1910, shows the fashionable interior of the 'Horse and Groom's' dining saloon. The proprietor, W.H.Jamieson, advertises Luncheons, Dinners, Teas, Suppers with chops and steaks from the Silver Grill.

Flying Horse
Hotel,
Nottingham.

ESTABLISHED
1483.

TELEPHONE
4164-5.

TELEGRAMS:
" Flying,
Nottingham."

HOTEL ENTRANCE.

8. Flying Horse - Poultry, Nottingham. An advertising card for the hotel claims it was established in 1483. All the sadder, therefore, that the ornate interior with horses' heads prominent should have been lost for ever. Card sent from Nottingham in April 1911 : *'Arrived 6.30pm. Called in Derby this afternoon'*.

9. Flying Horse - Poultry, Nottingham. Recent developments might have spared the exterior of the 'Flying Horse' but the plush interior illustrated here on this card has been sadly lost for ever.

10. Old Dog and Partridge - Lower Parliament Street, Nottingham. The head of the march is just drawing level with the pub which sold locally produced Shipstone Ales. Built during the First World War, it stood almost opposite a pub of the same name. Notice how the streets are empty of traffic.

The Talbot, Nottingham.
The Palatial Corridor leading to the King's Hall.

11. The Talbot - Chapel Bar, Nottingham. This pre-First World War card, published by H. & J. West, Ramsgate, gives some indication of the opulence of the interior of 'The Talbot' - a marked contrast to the 'spit and sawdust' reputation of part of the establishment in later times.

THEATRE SQUARE, NOTTINGHAM

12. Clarendon Hotel - Theatre Square, Nottingham. Strategically situated between the Hippodrome and the Theatre Royal, the 'Clarendon Hotel' served a large and varied clientele. It had periods under the names 'The Rufford' and 'The County Hotel'. It fell victim to redevelopment in the area when the Royal Concert Hall was built.

THE
WHEATSHEAF
INN

BOBBERS MILL
NOTTINGHAM
PHONE 734211

Mine Hosts

MR & MRS R.N. POLLOCK

WEDDINGS
and
PARTIES CATERED FOR
SHIPSTONES ALES

13. The Wheatsheaf Inn - Bobbers Mill, Nottingham. An unusual advertising card for this Shipstones Ales public house, run by Mr and Mrs R.N.Pollock when this card was published in the 1950s. The aerial view shows the pub's strange situation on an island surrounded by roads. The postcard was sent to Mrs Hobson of the 'Albion Inn', Lenton saying *'Thanks for giving us such a lovely holiday. Everything perfect'*.

14. The Beacon - Aspley. Designed by Bailey and Eberfin of Nottingham in the Tudor style with oak half timbering to the upper storey, this pub on Aspley Lane was opened in 1936. Its name derives from the sign given in times past to warn of the approach of enemy invaders.

15. Grove Hotel - Daybrook. A card in the 'Clumber' series, posted to Ockbrook in July 1908, shows the 'Grove Hotel' situated on Mansfield Road. It was originally built in the mid-19th century but was purchased by the local Home Brewery in 1897 for £7,000. They obviously wasted no time in decking it out in their own advertising slogans.

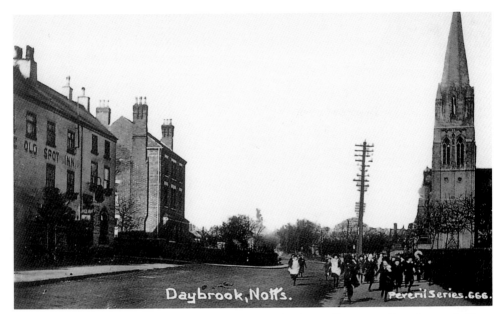

16. Old Spot Inn - Daybrook. Situated close to the Home Brewery, this pub was built in 1785. The derivation of the name is lost in the mists of time, though 'Old Spot' was a prized local racehorse in the reign of William IV, and the Duke of Newcastle also owned a horse of this name at the end of the 17th century. Card in the 'Peveril Series', No.666.

17. Four Bells Inn - Woodborough. This card was published by Spree soon after the pub was built in 1926. It replaced an earlier pub of the same name in the village. The name derives from the four bells to be found in the belfry of St Swithins, which can just be seen to the right of the picture.

18. The Mason's Arms - Hucknall. The narrow High Street in Hucknall leading up to the market place actually features two public houses: 'The Mason's Arms' to the right and the 'Bryon's Rest' to the left - both have disappeared over the last 40 years as the road has been widened and the buildings cleared and replaced.

19. The Lord Clyde - Kimberley. Kimberley, with at one time two breweries, Hardys and Hansons, has more than its fair share of public houses. The 'Lord Clyde' stands facing the War Memorial and takes its name from the Commander in Chief of the Army in India at the time of the Mutiny (1857). This card in the 'Rex Series' (No. 1403), published in the 1920s, was posted to Doncaster in September 1925.

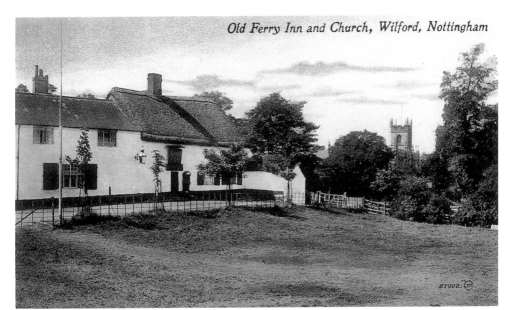

Old Ferry Inn and Church, Wilford, Nottingham

20. Ferry Boat Inn - Wilford. This building dates from the 14th century when it was a farmhouse. It has previously been known as 'Wilford Coffee House and Tea Gardens' and 'The Punch Bowl'. Its present name is explained by its close proximity to the River Trent.

HIGH ROAD, BEESTON.

21. The Greyhound Inn and The Durham Ox - Beeston. Two adjacent public houses in the High Road at Beeston. The horse and cart is drawn up outside the early 19th century 'Durham Ox', while beyond it is the even earlier 'Greyhound' which was built in 1741. Card posted in 1910 to Sefton Park in Liverpool.

22. Charlton Arms - Chilwell. Situated on High Road, Chilwell, this mock Tudor pub takes its name from a long established local family. Nicholas Charlton was resident in Chilwell Hall in 1620, whilst 200 years later Colonel Thomas Charlton lived there. This card was sent from nearby Beeston in May 1951.

23. Sherwin Arms - Bramcote. The 1930s mock-Tudor building illustrated on this anonymously published card replaced an earlier pub of the same name which was demolished for road widening. Over the porch can be seen the family arms of John Sherwin, a local landowner, who in 1805 built Bramcote Hills House in a nearby park.

Ye old Nottingham Road   STAPLEFORD   (Copyright)

24. Warren Arms - Stapleford. Local company Poole and Son published this rural view of the 'Warren Arms' during the Edwardian period. The name comes from the Warren family who resided at Stapleford Hall from 1675. The most famous family member was Sir John Borlase Warren, who gave his name to other pubs locally. Posted locally in April 1909. *'The weather is grand; we had a hearty welcome'*, wrote Alice.

25. The Old Cross Inn - Stapleford. This 'Rex' Series card can be dated as after 1928 when the Old Cross, from which the pub takes its name, was moved from its position in the road outside the pub to the safety of the churchyard. The inn began as one of three cottages and was converted to beer selling soon after 1860.

26. Bricklayers Arms - Ruddington. The 'Bricklayers Arms' was opened on High Street in the 1860s. It is one of seven pubs in Ruddington, and is seen here on a 1960s card which contains a fine selection of cars from the period.

27. Red Lion - Costock. The small village of Costock, close to East Leake, boasts a pair of public houses. The 'Red Lion' seen here on a 1950s card published by A.W.Bourne looks very different to the Edwardian 'Red Lion' at Costock featured in volume 1 of *Nottinghamshire Inns and Pubs*.

28. Sun Inn - Gotham. Situated facing the village pump, the 'Sun Inn' was originally three cottages which have been knocked into one. It has been an Inn since the 1840s.

29. Salutation Inn - Keyworth. A 1960s card by A.W.Bourne of Leicester captures a view of Keyworth's oldest public house.

517P   THE GRIFFIN

LUMTREE, NOTTS,

30. The Griffin Inn - Plumtree. Standing in the centre of the village of Plumtree, 'The Griffin Inn' was built by the Burnside family in 1843. This card in W.H.Smith's 'Clumber' Series (No.517P) captures a group of boys playing marbles on the road between the village school and the pub.

Stragglethorpe Road, Cotgrave.

31. Manvers Arms - Cotgrave. Facing the village post office, the 'Manvers Arms', seen here on a card postally used in 1944, has a long history. During the Napoleonic wars, a company of White's Dragoons was stationed there.

"The Black Lion," Radcliffe-on-Trent

32. Black Lion - Radcliffe-on-Trent. Although this building only dates from 1928, there had been a 'Black Lion' in Radcliffe for many years previously, situated on Main Street. This inn, selling Home Ales, is situated on the original village pinfold site. Card published by A.W.Bourne of Leicester.

LONG ACRE, BINGHAM, NOTTS.

COPYRIGHT, J. S. & S.

33. Wheatsheaf Inn and Vaults Inn - Bingham. It is surprising how many places had inns close together in Edwardian times. This J.Sands & Sons card posted in 1917 shows Long Acre in Bingham where the 'Wheatsheaf Inn' on the left faced the 'Vaults Inn' on the right.

THE MARKET PLACE, BINGHAM.

706 / 26

34. Crown Inn - Bingham. This card, posted from the village in April 1912, shows the 'Crown Inn' facing the Market Place and its impressive Butter Cross. At this time, the licensee was the quaintly named Sam F.Blood who sold Home brewed ales and advertised *'Good accommodation and teas'*. This building was demolished in 1966 and replaced by a new 'Crown Inn' on the same site.

35. Unicorn Inn - Langar. Most small villages had an inn during the Edwardian period and the South Notts village of Langar was no exception. The card was sent from Barnstone (about a mile from Langar) in 1907.

36. The Plough - Cropwell Butler. This inn dates from the nineteenth century : at one time it had a thatched roof. Its oldest section is in fact furthest from the road. The façade remains remarkably similar today, though a large new porch has been added onto the side. Postcard published by Spree, and posted to Melton Mowbray in May 1928.

37. Royal Oak - Car Colston. This 200 year old pub allegedly boasts a pair of ghosts - a Roman centurion who inhabits the cellars and a Victorian gentleman patrolling the bar. Today it still dominates the green, though you're more likely to find coaches and cars in an enlarged car park. The tree on the right no longer stands, and the pub sign and main entrance have changed markedly.

38. Lord Nelson - Burton Joyce. For many years the Burton Joyce Feast took place each October in front of the 'Lord Nelson'. Its position close to the river explains its previous names 'The Swan and Salmon' (1809), 'The White Swan' (1811) and 'The Sign of the Swan' (1826).

UNICORN HOTEL. GUNTHORPE. NOTTS.

39. Unicorn Hotel - Gunthorpe. Another inn to be found on the banks of the River Trent. There have been buildings on this site for over 300 years, and this pub has had various names including 'The Ferry House'. The name 'Unicorn', which comes from James I's coat of arms, was first used in 1824. Card in the 'Peveril Real Photo' series.

The Magna Charta, Lowdham

40. Magna Charta - Lowdham. The photographer on this 1927 postally used card has managed to get an empty road on this view towards Thurgarton and Southwell. The pub, advertising Hanson's Kimberley ales, was built prior to 1844 and takes its name from the famous event in 1215 when King John was forced to sign the Magna Carta by the Barons at Runnymede.

The Crown Inn, Rolleston, No. 1456.

41. Crown Inn - Rolleston. Handily placed in the village centre, close to Southwell Racecourse, the 'Crown Inn', dating from the 1830s, is widely known for the large tree with an opening in its trunk, through which newlyweds used to pass in order to obtain good luck. Card by C.& A.G.Lewis, posted at Kelham in 1921.

High St, Collingham.

42. Royal Oak - Collingham. Seen here in more tranquil times about to be passed by a horse and cart, the 'Royal Oak' was built jutting out into, and narrowing, the High Street. At one time it was also known as 'Hoe's Railway Hotel'.

Newcastle Arms & Ferry House, North Muskham, Newark.

43. Newcastle Arms - North Muskham. As can be seen from this card sent from nearby Newark on 14th May, 1907, the 'Newcastle Arms' stood on the River Trent. It was a convenient ferry point to Holme on the opposite bank. Built in 1692, the inn was re-christened 'The Muskham Ferry' in 1980.

44. Rose and Crown - Balderton. By the 1920s Balderton contained four pubs of which the 'Rose and Crown', seen here, was one. It boasted a skittle alley, which at one time doubled as the village fire station. Close by were the older 'Turk's Head' and 'Cock Inn'. Postcard published by Frith of Reigate.

45. Elephant and Castle - Norwell. Two pubs for the price of one! The little girl is standing outside the now demolished 'Elephant and Castle Inn' (John William Cook, licensee) whilst down at the end of the road can be seen the 'Plough Inn' and its adjacent shop.

46. Black Swan - Edwinstowe. Built about 600 years ago, the 'Black Swan' is the oldest inn in the village. At the time of this card, A.Fletcher was the licensee. Just up the High Street can be seen the larger premises of the 'Jug and Glass', which was built at the turn of the century.

47. The Dukeries Hotel - Edwinstowe. The mock-Tudor style Dukeries hotel was built by Mansfield Brewery in 1897. It suffered extensive fire damage in February 1929, but was soon restored to its former splendour.

48. White Lion - Blidworth. The Sherwood Photographic Company of Mansfield produced this card showing the 'White Lion'. The first building on the right was a saddler's shop run by the Maxfield brothers. Next to it was Wightman's butcher's shop. Between these two, up to Edwardian times, was another pub, the 'Red Lion'.

49. Plough Inn - New Ollerton. New Ollerton grew up to serve the miners at New Ollerton Colliery which opened in September 1926. The 'Plough Inn' was one such new facility, opening at this time. Note the petrol pump at the front of the inn. The card was posted to Pilsley in August 1927.

50. The Squinting Cat - Clipstone. This 1950s view by A.W.Bourne (Leicester) shows what must be a leading candidate for the pub with the most unusual name in Nottinghamshire. It refers to the cat behaviour researches of Dr Leyhausen at a German university. The link to Clipstone is unknown.

51. Dog and Duck - Clipstone. Old Clipstone village is the site of this pub, whose building dates from early in the 19th century. This card by the Doncaster Rotophoto Co Ltd was postally used in 1921.

52. Half Moon Inn - Retford. The imposing Town Hall takes pride of place on this Valentine's card, but the white building next to it advertising Worksop Fine Ales is the 'Half Moon Inn'. This building was substantially altered, especially the façade, in 1930 although it retained its name.

Queen's Hotel, Retford.
H. L. Dewick Propr.

TEL 64

53. Queen's Hotel - Retford. This card, published by W.H.Smith in their 'Aldwych' series, shows the 'Queen's Hotel' which was built on Queen Street near the railway station to meet the needs of rail travellers. It also catered for the motor car, advertising the fact that it had a garage pit. The proprietor, H.L.Dewick, was the owner of one of the first cars in Retford.

Canal Bridge. Clayworth.

J.T.

54. White Hart Inn - Clayworth. Picturesquely situated by the Chesterfield Canal, the 'White Hart Inn' dates from the beginning of the 19th century. The Worksop and Retford Boat Club bought the premises as their headquarters in June 1969. Card posted to Pontefract in 1912.

Market Place Tuxford. 237. 12.

55. Newcastle Arms - Tuxford. This Hotel, seen here on a card posted in 1923, takes its name from the Duke of Newcastle, the local Lord of the Manor. It is advertising the local Worksop Ales. Published by the Doncaster Rotophoto Co., it was posted to an address in Nottingham's Meadows in 1926.

WALESBY 6

56. Carpenters Arms - Walesby. When this view was taken prior to the First World War, the publican was Alfred Sharp, who advertised 'accommodation for cyclists'.

57. Butchers Arms - Laneham. Card No. 28 in the 'Woolass Series' shows the 'Butcher's Arms' at Laneham, reputed to be over 400 years old and to have been named after the butcher's shop which use to stand in the pub grounds. The card's writer, John says *'I am send you a photo of our shop'*.

58. Durham Ox - Wellow. The quaint village of Wellow near Ollerton with its village green and maypole has two pubs. Seen here is the original 'Durham Ox' with a horse and cart just passing the entrance. The card was sent by someone living at the Post Office in Wellow.

59. The Grey Horses - Carlton in Lindrick. The original 'Grey Horses' was in South Carlton and acted as a staging post for coaches. This inn was closed under influence from a strong non-conformist tee-total movement but the business was soon re-established in the building seen in the picture.

60. Jug and Glass - Langwith. The London Stores, Langwith published this card of the 'Jug and Glass'. Built of local stone, this former coaching inn is situated facing the village stream and cross.

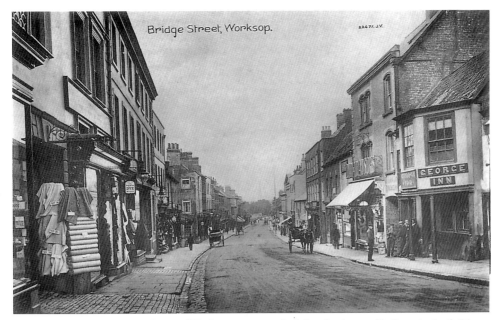

61. George Inn - Worksop. Worksop was noted for its inns. At the start of this century, it had 64 licensed houses of which the 17th century 'George Inn' was one of the oldest. At one time the local court met there but sadly the building is no longer with us. Card published by Valentine's of Dundee and posted to Norwich in May 1917.

62. Fox and Hounds - Walkeringham. When this unattributed postcard was published in the early 1920s, the 'Fox and Hounds' was run by Mrs Mary Ann Hemstock.

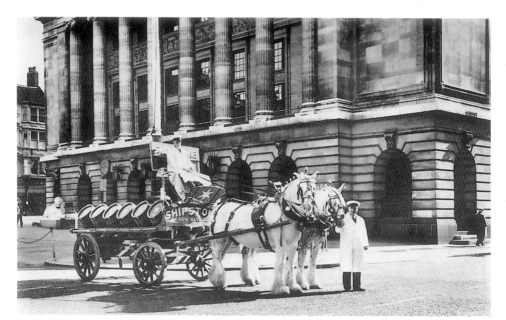

63. Shipstones - Dray Horse. James Shipstone and Sons Ltd., Star Brewery, Nottingham published this card to advertise their Draught Beers *'drawn straight from the wood'* - Many of us have fond memories of the horses and carts delivering round the city until fairly recent times. The horses and dray are shown outside Nottingham's Council House.

64. Delivery Vehicles, Holes Brewery - Newark. James Hole and Co Ltd. worked from the Castle Brewery, Albert Street, Newark. This is part of their fleet of delivery vehicles thought to date from the 1930s. Holes lost its independence in 1967 when Courage Brewery took it over.